—— the ——
RESILIENT
mind

A FIELD GUIDE TO A **HEALTHIER** WAY OF **LIFE**

Christmas Hutchinson

The Resilient Mind

Written by Christmas Hutchinson

Edited by Peter Gerardo

Cover Design by Gerry P. Aguelo

DEDICATION

To my mother Ann Hutchinson-

Thank you for loving me from day one even
when it wasn't your responsibility to do so.

You are the epitome of resilience and without
you, this book would not exist.

CONTENTS

Introduction

On a brisk October day, I sat quietly in my doctor's office, waiting for my name to be called. This was no ordinary trip to the OB/GYN. I was making a special trip to learn the results of the tissue biopsy they had taken from my left breast the week before. My mind was racing. With my nine-year marriage ending in divorce just a week earlier, I had entirely too much to process. The divorce was fresh on my mind, and now I might have a health problem – a *serious* health problem.

The door opened and the doctor appeared.

"Hi Christmas. Thanks for coming in. We received the results of your biopsy," she said in her usual chipper voice.

"Oh good. What did you find?" I asked nervously.

"Well, blah, blah, blah, blah, blah, blah, blah ... early stages of cancer," is what I heard.

"I'm sorry. Did you say I have pre-cancer?"

"No, Christmas, the mass found in your breast is a tumor and needs to be removed by a surgeon," she said in a matter-of-fact tone.

My voice trembling, I asked, "Will I have to take chemotherapy?"

"Yes," she said, handing me a stack of

literature about breast cancer. I stood and walked out of the office in complete shock, contemplating my life up to that point. On the drive home, my mind raced even faster. "What do I tell my mom? What do I tell my job? What do I tell my friends? Will I lose my hair? Will I lose weight? Will they remove my breasts? Am I going to die?"

Because I'm a problem-solver, I set priorities. I would: (1) tackle the physical health issue; and then (2) tackle the mental health issues stemming from the divorce. It wouldn't be easy, but with patience and faith, I knew I'd eventually enjoy happier, cancer-free days.

Thanks to these physical and emotional blows, I learned that to be resilient in tough times you need a certain set of tools. In this book, I share the tools I've learned and used – tools that keep me bouncing back; tools that have made me a better person than when misfortune first came knocking on my door. I was inspired to write this book because I learned that the one constant in life is that there will always be reversals, and it's better to be prepared for them than to hope they never happen. Eventually, they *will* happen.

How to read this book

The chapters in this book don't have to be read consecutively. You can read them in any order. I encourage you to refer to this book whenever you're looking for a tool to help you through a rough patch. I wish I'd owned such a book when I was 25 years old. I hope you find it helpful. For additional tips on resilience, please visit my website: www.simply-resilient.com.

— 1 —

Self-Preservation
is Paramount to Resilience

"Chrissy, not everyone loves the way you do, and not everyone will be able to love you the way you need to be loved."
—*Ann Hutchinson, my mother*

We live in a time when "self-care" is trendy, but rightfully so. We, as a culture, are feeling the effects of stress. Burnout and mental illness are increasingly common. If you do a Google search on self-care, more than 107 million results will pop up. Many of the articles and blogs offer tips on meditation, keeping a gratitude journal or taking a nice bath to unwind. These are great tips. I've used them. However, I've noticed that one key thing is missing in the self-care movement: *self-love*. Self-love is the foundation of self-preservation. Practicing all the self-care in the world will take you only so far if you don't love yourself.

My first lesson in self-preservation came when I separated from my husband. When I reached this decision, I was at an all-time low. I was traveling every week for work, and was very active with my sorority on weekends. When I *was* home, I was unable to find a refuge in my husband. Instead, he continually complained about my lifestyle and how it wasn't working for him. Needless to say, this didn't make me feel better about myself.

As I reflect on that time, I wonder how I didn't have a nervous breakdown. I literally felt trapped. I hated my life, and resented myself for creating it. Ironically, by the standards of our culture, I had a wonderful life! I was married to a decent man, had a big house in the suburbs, worked for one of the world's largest professional services firms, and stayed in fancy hotels every week.

But something told me to walk away from my marriage and my home in order to figure this whole thing out, so I left and moved to a place of my own. The marriage had gotten so bad that fixing it while living under the same roof wasn't going to work, especially because my ex-husband couldn't fathom that my feelings were *real*. Leaving gave me space and time to think about how I'd arrived at such a low point.

As it turned out, retracing that journey would take another year and half.

It wasn't until my divorce was final and I'd been diagnosed with cancer that I came to understand the meaning of self-love.

I reached this understanding the day my ex-husband called to tell me that he'd just visited a friend who also had cancer. His friend's cancer was more serious than mine, as he had to be hospitalized while receiving treatment.

I will never forget the thoughts that rolled around my mind after the call. I was so hurt. I understood that we were no longer married. However, we'd known each other for a third of our lives. Given all the history between us, I expected that he would be there for *me* while I endured this difficult time.

Then I asked myself, "Why is it so important to receive acknowledgement and care from him?" The answer I came up with was, "That's how *I* would treat someone who was dealing with an illness."

I called my mother and expressed my disappointment with my ex-husband. In response, she told me something very valuable.

"Chrissy, not everyone loves the way you do, and not everyone will be able to love you the way you need to be loved."

These words put into perspective all of my disparate thoughts about love and how I valued myself. I'd always believed that if I showed love to others, it would be automatically returned in the same way. And here I was: feeling bitter and hurt that I wasn't receiving the love I deserved. Why did I think it was someone else's responsibility to love me? More important, why was I expending love on *others* before considering myself?

These questions helped me discover the lack of value that I placed on myself. They made me realize that I needed to change – to love myself harder than I'd been loving the other people in my life. I realized that I had very little self-worth, which was the reason I was feeling so bad about not receiving the love I expected from an ex-husband.

I decided that I would transfer all the love I was giving everyone else to myself.

Once I did this, my life changed. The bitterness from the marriage dissipated, and I created a new relationship with myself.

Getting to where I am now took time. It took many days of affirmations – of telling myself "I am valuable and worthy" – and forgiving myself for not valuing myself in the first place. I also had to draw boundaries around people who brought negative energy into my space (aka, "toxic people") and practice a form of "self-worth maintenance."

I go into more detail about self-care throughout this book, but some of the "Go-To" maintenance activities I employ include meditation, "resetting" and exercise.

Self-Preservation + resilience

Being proactive about self-preservation is key. If you don't love yourself, you're more likely to put yourself in situations where you're used and abused. People will think that it's okay to treat you poorly because you don't seem to think that you deserve better. Have you ever heard the saying, "What you allow will continue"?

Practicing self-love and self-care helps you bounce back faster when you experience setbacks. For example, I practice gratitude as a form of self-care. Whenever I feel depressed, I write down the things I am grateful for. This immediately improves my mood. If I didn't include gratitude in my practice, I would succumb to prolonged states of depression. Practicing gratitude helps to cut that sadness short.

Get started today:

- ❖ Read chapters 2, 3 and 4 for more details about my "Go-To" self-care techniques.
- ❖ Develop some affirmations on self-worth. My favorite is: *I am smart. I am beautiful. I am valuable.* I say this affirmation daily – in the morning while getting ready for the day and at night until I fall asleep. I also repeat these affirmations *aloud*, so I can hear them.
- ❖ Start saying "no" to things you really don't want to do. For example, if a friend invites you out, and you're tired or just don't feel like going, don't feel bad about saying "no."

— 2 —

Meditate Regularly

"Quiet the mind and the soul will speak."
— *Ma Jaya Sati Bhagavati*

When people used to tell me that they mediated, I could never wrap my mind around what they were doing. How could spending 10 minutes being quiet change my life? In fact, I thought that spending 10 minutes doing absolutely nothing was impossible.

After separating from my husband, however, I noticed that I was holding on to some bitterness. I would catch myself replaying the same "memory reel" of behaving like a great person and wondering why I wasn't appreciated. This bitterness kept me up at night, and my feelings about the breakup came up in almost every conversation. It consumed me.

But what could I do? Was this negativity my new normal?

While undergoing cancer treatment, I was also trying to survive depression triggered by the divorce. The depression was so bad that I couldn't sleep (and it didn't help that a common side effect of chemotherapy is insomnia). I also suffered from anxiety over whether the cancer treatment would work – and even if it did, was I destined to later die as a single "cat lady?" Because I lived alone, nobody else knew what I was going through, and I would put on a show of happiness whenever friends came to visit.

One day, while talking with a friend about his struggle with depression and negative thoughts, he suggested I try an iPhone app called *Headspace*. The app features a series of guided meditations that you can do for as little as five minutes.

I was at home on a Saturday when I tried the app. In various articles I've read, the authors advise that you get to a quiet place and in a comfortable position, so I chose to lay down on my bed. After browsing through the meditations, I chose the shortest one I could find. I didn't think I could commit to being still and undistracted for more than five minutes.

I pressed play and followed the narrator's instructions to focus on my breathing while a mellow song played in the background. After I was done, I thought, "Wow. I *do* feel somewhat relaxed." But I still wasn't convinced that meditation would change my life.

Nevertheless, I decided to meditate for another 13 days.

I started reading more about meditation, and saw that many articles claimed that prolonged meditation produces better results. After 14 days, my life wasn't completely changed, but I *was* calmer. Situations that would ordinarily irritate me (for example, D.C. traffic) didn't bother me as much. That convinced me to continue meditating.

After practicing meditation every day, twice a day, for about a year, I began to become bored with it. I convinced myself that I was all better, so I stopped. A couple of months later, though, I noticed changes in my temperament. I began to blow every negative interaction out of proportion, which would kill my mood for long periods. I couldn't put my finger on how I started to become negative until I asked myself what was different about my life. Then I remembered: I'd stopped my daily meditation practice.

I added the practice back into my life, and noticed that my general outlook and interactions became more positive. All the little things that had started annoying me again no longer bothered me. This made me a believer in the power of meditation to dramatically improve one's life.

Our mind processes hundreds of

thousands of bits of information every day, most of which is noise. Just as you clean your house and wash your clothes, it is necessary to cleanse your mind of daily clutter. Meditation is the best way to do this.

According to a study conducted by Yale University, meditation decreases activity in the part of the brain where mind wandering and self-referential thoughts occur.[i] A study by the National Institutes of Health (NIH) showed that meditation over an eight-week period improved anxiety and stress among the participants.[ii]

A great way to get started is to download a guided meditation app such as *Headspace* and try the five-minute meditations. Another resource is YouTube. I particularly like Louise Hay's *morning meditation* and *evening meditation*. Try it for a week, but make sure to journal your experience so you can document any changes in your thoughts and outlook on life.

[i] Brewer, Judson. (2011 December 13) *Meditation experience is associated with differences in default mode network activity and connectivity*. Retrieved from www.pnas.org
[ii] Goyal, M., Singh, S (2014 March) *Meditation programs for psychological stress and well-being: systemic review and meta analysis*. Retrieved from www.ncbi.nlm.nih.gov

If you want to do something more on your own, I recommend buying a book that has meditation prompts. Meditation prompts are pre-written meditations directed at areas of life that may cause you anxiety. I received one as a gift: Louise Hay's *Meditations to Heal Your Life*. It contains a series of meditation prompts that can help with all areas of your life, including career, finances, love and finding courage.

Meditation + resiliency

In my experience, meditation builds peace of mind and confidence. After meditating for the last few years, I have more confidence, little to no anxiety and improved self-esteem. I was able to measure this by revisiting my journal entries from five years ago. When I read the entries, I couldn't recognize the person I was back then. Most entries reflected the negative thoughts I had about myself and my lack of certainty of what I should be doing. By contrast, when I review journal entries from the last year or so, I notice that they are more contemplative and always have a theme of moving forward.

I still have bad days when it comes to my

mood, but since I began meditating regularly, they are *far* less frequent.

Get started today:

❖ Download a meditation app like Headspace.
❖ Commit to meditating at least five minutes a day for the next seven days.
❖ Journal about your experience.

— 3 —

Don't Avoid the Doctor

"If you care about your contributions to the world, you'll care for yourself."
—*Brendon Burchard*

If you have health insurance, there's no reason *not* to see a doctor at least once a year. It's imperative to be proactive about your health, not just reactive. Although I've always visited a physician regularly, I discovered my cancer because of the education my doctor gave me about self-examination.

This isn't to say that being reactive is always a bad thing. You should also schedule an appointment when you feel pain or notice something different about your body. If you feel something is "off," react! If you can't get an immediate appointment with your regular physician, go to urgent care.

Here are two stories that convinced me to become more proactive.

The first involves a college mate who was feeling pain in his lower abdomen. He ignored it. He went to work, picked up his kids from school and went about his routine despite excruciating pain. He did this for several days.

Eventually, he collapsed and was rushed

to the emergency room. The doctors did everything they could to save him, but he didn't make it.

It was later discovered that his spleen had ruptured days earlier. After learning this, the doctors told his wife that there was *no way* he hadn't been in pain, given how suddenly he passed away. His body warned him that something was seriously wrong. He could have saved himself. Instead, he pushed through the pain until it was too late.

He was 31 years old and left behind two children and a wife.

I know that when it's our time to go, it's our time. But that didn't have to be *his* time.

This tragedy was a lesson to me: when you notice a problem with your body, see a doctor *immediately*.

The second story hits especially close to home. You see, I also lost my father because he decided to avoid the doctor.

Four years before his death, my father had an artificial heart valve implanted. Unfortunately, he was inconsistent about taking the blood thinners needed to reduce clotting in the device. One October day, my father experienced chest pains. After many hours of coping with the pain, he finally agreed to go to the emergency room. The E.R. physician told my dad that he had blockages in his heart valve that needed to be cleared via angioplasty. My dad was (understandably) frightened of this major procedure, and delayed having it for a few more hours. The delay proved fatal. My dad had three clots that needed to be removed. He died as the doctor was clearing the final clot.

These experiences made such a profound impression that when I discovered the lump in my breast, I scheduled an appointment with my doctor within one hour. I didn't want to wait until it became blindingly obvious that something was wrong. I saw my doctor on a Friday, and she scheduled a biopsy for the following Monday. Three days later, the biopsy came back positive for cancer. I was not about to roll the dice with my health. I found out I had cancer at 5:00 p.m. on a Wednesday, and called the surgeon at 9:00 a.m. the next morning.

When you get bad news about your health, you have a choice: face it, or let fear take over and avoid it. Avoidance is not a solution. If you avoid reality, you risk turning a treatable problem into an irreversible disaster.

Physical health + resiliency

Before my health scare, I often heard the Steve Adler quote, "You can have all the riches in the world, but if you don't have your health, you have nothing." After experiencing what cancer treatment involves – being sliced up, poisoned and burned (surgery, chemotherapy and radiation) – I came to appreciate that quote.

Being unable to perform simple tasks – walking, sleeping and keeping down food – made me appreciate my health in a way few people do. It also gave me the will to fight for my health. I now knew how much better feeling "normal" was, and I wanted to feel that way again.

Get started today:

❖ Check in with yourself. Ask yourself the following questions:
  • Is something happening with your health that you haven't consulted a doctor about?
  • Are you feeling tired, no matter how much rest you get?
  • Do you experience aches in your body that you can't explain?
  • Have there been major changes in your body that you can't explain – for example, rapid weight loss, frequent urination or changes to your skin?
  • Has it been more than two years since you had a complete physical exam, as well as blood tests?

If you answered yes to any of these questions, schedule an appointment with a doctor. At the very least, you will have peace of mind and a plan for your health going forward.

— 4 —

Spend Time Resetting

"Sometimes, you need to be alone, not to be lonely,
but to enjoy your free time being yourself."
—*Unknown*

Taking time for yourself can sometimes seem impossible. It doesn't help that our culture tends to equate success with being busy. According to a study by Harvard University, participants perceived busy people as high status, thus the belief that hard work leads to more opportunities to be successful.[iii] Given this perception, it's no wonder so many people are burned out.

These days, the entire family is busy. Many jobs that once required 40 hours a week are now creeping up to 50 hours. (When work email is attached to your phone, this eats up even more time.) And if work isn't enough, there are also extracurricular activities such as

---

[iii] Belleza, Silvia, Paharia, Neeru, Keinan, Anat. (2016 December 15) *Research: Why Americans are so impressed by busyness.* Retrieved from www.hbr.org

church, professional organizations and family obligations.

I used to be one of those people who proudly said I was busy when people asked what I'd been up to. I used to keep myself busy for two reasons: (1) I didn't want to face my own thoughts; and (2) I believed that *not* being busy meant I was wasting my life.

A couple of years ago, however, I reached a breaking point. I was traveling every week for my consulting job and volunteering for special projects at work. I was president of my sorority chapter, planning a 200-person luncheon, while also trying to manage my personal relationships. Juggling all these activities sent me into a depression. I'm usually an upbeat person, so when I'm depressed, people notice. So people noticed that I wasn't exercising, that I was stress eating and that I was being a bitch. Thankfully, these people called my attention to the changes in my mood. They helped me examine my life and determine what was bringing me to such a negative place.

To help *myself*, I listed all the activities I was doing and rated their importance on a scale from 1 – 10 in terms of the impact they had on my life. I then asked myself two questions: (1) "Is this activity something I saw

28

myself doing when I set goals for myself 10 years ago"; and (2) "Will I look back 20 years from now and be proud that I spent so much time on this activity?" I also analyzed the activities in terms of which ones were producing the most meaningful results.

This gave me a clear picture of what I needed to remove from my life. I also discovered the importance of periodically performing this exercise to keep things in perspective. The most valuable part of the process was realizing that I had to slow down to make these evaluations. This caused me to become proactive about scheduling time to *reset*. I do this by scheduling a few hours, or an entire day, every month for "down time" – time to think about the Big Picture. I either spend the time thinking about my life or simply escaping from day-to-day rigors to do what I want.

Spending time on yourself gives you the reset you need to manage all the complexities and interactions of life. For example, recall how you feel when you return from a vacation or a three-day weekend. I hope you said "refreshed." If not, the first thing you should do after reading this chapter is schedule some time for yourself. When you do, make sure you devote the time entirely to your own thoughts. Ideally, you should do this at least once a month, but I know that's not always possible. If it's not, schedule a reset at least once every three months. If you think four times a year is excessive, you *really* need a reset. Four days out of 365 will not sabotage your productivity. In fact, it will make you more productive. Schedule reset time on your calendar – just like you would any other event in your life.

If you're worried you can't make time for yourself because you have kids and a spouse, enlist your spouse's help. Agree on dates when *each* of you can take some "me" time. If you don't have a spouse but you have children, ask a friend if they can care for the kids while you enjoy a reset.

Resetting + resiliency

Taking time to reset helps reduce the likelihood of burnout and prevent a host of mental health issues, including depression and anxiety. Also, taking time to reset gives you the opportunity to evaluate your actions and decide if they need to change or if you want to "stay the course." This is important. We often get so lost in day-to-day activities that, before we know it, several months have passed while we were on "auto pilot."

Get started today

❖ Add three hours per week of "me time" to your schedule to spend any way you want – reading a book, watching your favorite show, taking a walk, getting your nails done, or just thinking and reflecting.

❖ Schedule the "me time" in one-hour blocks.

❖ After one month of scheduling "me time" for three hours a week, try increasing the number of hours to six per week. That's almost one hour a day for yourself.

— 5 —

Find an Exercise you Like

"Training gives us an outlet for suppressed energies created by stress and thus tones the spirit just as exercise conditions the body."
—*Arnold Schwarzenegger*

You only get one body in this life, and it has to last a long time.

What you put in your body is one component of staying healthy, but exercise has great benefits that will keep you going. According to *Harvard Health*, exercising regularly can help boost your immune system,[iv] which is vital to resilience.

Exercise also helps to keep your heart healthy. The American Heart Association suggests moderate physical activity, 150 minutes per week, to improve overall cardiovascular health.[v]

[iv] (2014 September) *How to Boost your Immune System: Helpful ways to strengthen your immune system and fight disease.* Retrieved from www.health.harvard.edu
[v] (2018 April 18) *American Heart Association Recommendations for Physical Activity in Adults.* Retrieved from www.heart.org

If you aren't exercising now, it's going to be more difficult to move around when you're older. According to Johns Hopkins Medicine Health Library, adults who are physically active reduce their risk of falls and improve their ability to do daily activities.[vi]

I grew up athletic. I swam, played soccer and danced. When I got to college, I began doing those things less and less often because I no longer had the structure I had when I was living with my parents. I quit being a lifeguard and adopted a routine of straightening my hair. (Working out after straightening my hair ruined my hair style, which was very important to me at the time.) Eventually, I stopped exercising altogether. I would go to the gym sporadically, but I never had a routine – and it showed in my waistline and my mood. Years passed before I got tired of how I looked and decided that I needed to reduce my stress levels.

I don't remember how I was introduced to it, but I started running. Until that time, I'd despised running my whole life. I remember my mom entering me in track during elementary

---

[vi] Johns Hopkins Medicine Health Library – Risk of Physical Inactivity. Retrieved from www.johnshopkinsmedicine.org

school, and I didn't like it. Nonetheless, I started training myself to run on a treadmill. One day, a friend asked if I wanted to run 5K and I agreed. The race was set for New Year's Day, and I thought it would be a good way to start the year. I ran/walked the full 3.1 miles. It took me 48 minutes to complete, but I didn't care. I was proud just to have finished. The next day, I was tired and sore, but I didn't care about that either. I had finished an actual race – something I never imagined I could do! The spark for running was ignited from that day forward, and I continued running 5Ks. I then graduated to a 10K and then half marathons. (I have yet to work up the nerve to run a full marathon.)

Running became my exercise. My goals became running the races.

Nowadays, I don't run as much because I found a new love: CrossFit. Thanks to CrossFit, I've built a stronger body, made new friends who I now call my family, and have the opportunity to challenge myself every day I step into the gym.

If you're intimidated by exercise, don't worry. You don't need to train for a marathon or join CrossFit. You just need to perform some activity for a minimum of 30 minutes a day, at least three times a week. When I was undergoing cancer treatment, my doctors encouraged me to take 15-minute (or longer) walks a few times a week. I always felt better afterwards. Otherwise, the chemotherapy infusions really wore me down.

The key to regular exercise is discovering what you enjoy. Until you find that activity, keep looking. I've tried all sorts of exercise – Zumba, Orange Theory Fitness, Insanity, CrossFit, yoga. I even hired a trainer and enlisted friends to go on walks and runs with me. In the process, I found what I love: running, CrossFit and yoga. It's not enough to say, "I don't do exercise" and leave it at that. Get off your butt and find what works for you!

To be healthy, you need to exercise at least three times a week. Even short walks are better than being sedentary.

For me, the biggest benefit of exercise is mood enhancement. I sometimes spend 15 minutes trying to talk myself out of exercising, but when I finally do it, I thank myself because I feel so amazing.

I think many people avoid exercise because they focus on the goals – the number of miles to be run or the weight to be lifted – not the process. You have to start somewhere, even if it's just walking around the block three times. Eventually, that three times will become four times, and before you know it, you'll be walking a mile without thinking about how intimidating that distance once seemed.

Find an exercise you like and find the time to do it. Most of us will look at our schedules and say we don't have time, but I've learned that there *is* always time to do what we want. If you work a lot of hours, take two 15-minute walks. Before you go to bed, do 20 sit-ups, 20 pushups and 20 squats. The next week, raise those numbers to 30. You have to start somewhere. Focus on the activity, not the goal. Fall in love with the *process* of exercise.

Exercise + resilience

Exercise is foundational to our health. Through my experience with cancer treatment, I have learned that if you don't have your health, you have nothing. If you aren't feeling well, you won't be able to do the things you love with the people you love.

If you don't exercise regularly, ask yourself: (1) "Am I always tired, and no matter what I do, I can't shake the fatigue?" (2) "Am I winded when I walk up a flight of stairs or do I avoid stairs altogether because I'm in no mood to exert that much energy?" (3) "Do I often experience back pain?"

If you answered *yes* to any of those questions, you need to engage in some kind of physical activity, whether it's a daily walk, stretching or yoga. Below are some resources you can use to launch an exercise regimen and start feeling better.

Get started now

- ❖ Commit to taking a 15-minute walk after lunch three times this week. If the weather is bad, walk up and down five flights of stairs 10 times.
- ❖ Challenge yourself to trying a new exercise – and feel free to bring a friend.
- ❖ Check out this article by *Harvard Health*: "Yoga - Benefits beyond the Mat."[vii]

[vii] (2015 February) *Yoga - Benefits Beyond the Mat.* Retrieved From www.health.harvard.edu

— 6 —

Practice Gratitude

"When gratitude becomes your default setting, life changes."
—*Nancy Leigh Demoss*

Practicing gratitude is one of my "Go-To" activities when I'm feeling down. I advise friends and family to do this when life becomes difficult. Focusing on the things that are going well, and feeling grateful for those experiences, puts me in a positive mood.

I began practicing gratitude to survive heartbreak and cancer treatment.

When I was diagnosed with cancer, my divorce was only seven days old. My emotional state was at an all-time low. I couldn't wrap my mind around why *I* had to endure all these horrible things at once. I questioned the decisions I'd made, and wondered what I'd done to deserve these ordeals. As much as I felt that life had dealt me a bad hand, these challenges were blessings in disguise. They offered an opportunity to focus on *living* instead of being bitter.

When I was diagnosed, I was hell bent on ensuring that I saw another year of life, so I started reading everything I could about surviving cancer. I read somewhere that having a positive outlook can help restore your health, and the article suggested that one way to remain positive is to focus on helping others. I took it to heart. I started writing "thank you" notes to friends and family. In the notes, I recalled the positive experiences I'd had with them and their impact on me. I felt validated in my efforts when, one day, I was at a conference and a speaker named Shawn Achor, the CEO of Goodthink and author of the *Happiness Advantage*, described a study performed in 2003 by the American Psychological Association. The study described how focusing on your blessings could have a positive effect on your emotional well-being.[viii]

To maintain my practice of gratitude, I have a gratitude jar. A pen and a pad of Post-it notes sits next to it. Whenever I feel grateful about something, no matter how small, I write it down and stuff it in the jar. For example: if I'm feeling low and a friend calls and cheers me up, I write down that experience and stuff it in the jar.

[viii] Emmons, Robert. McCullough, Michael. (2003, Vol. 84, No 2, 377-389) *Counting Blessings versus burdens: An experimental investigation of gratitude and subjective well-being in daily life.* Journal of Personality and Social Psychology

At the end of the year, I read the notes and reflect on all the great things that happened that year. I've been doing this for two years, and after each year, I empty the jar and start over. Doing this helps me feel good in the moment, and at the end of every year, I see how blessed I am. I also spend less time focusing on things that didn't go my way.

When I was undergoing cancer treatment, focusing on positive things kept me in a positive space. Living in this positive space brought hope to me and the people around me, which I believe is the reason I survived.

Gratitude + resilience

Spending time in gratitude is paramount to living a resilient life. When you spend more time being grateful for the things and people you have in your life, you inevitably will spend less time in sadness and despair. Keeping up a practice of gratitude will keep you moving forward and growing in your life. The moment you fall into the spiral of feeling lack and sadness is when life will stop progressing and you become consumed by the sadness. Resilience is all about bouncing back and continuing to move forward in spite of. Therefore, when you start to feel the sadness and despair creep in, turn your thoughts to gratitude because there is always something to be grateful for.

Get started now

- ❖ Check out Shawn Achor's 12-minute Ted Talk, "The Happy Secret to Better Work."
- ❖ For the next 7 days, write down at least five things or people you are grateful for – and why.
- ❖ Start a gratitude jar. All you need is a mason jar or an old jam jar and a pack of Post-It notes. For the next 30 days write one thing you are grateful for each day and stuff the note in the jar. When the 30 days are complete, go through and read the notes you stuffed in the jar the 30 days before.

7

Avoid Negative Self-talk

"You are only as good as the next thought of yourself."
—*Curtis Tyrone Jones*

We are our own worst critics. Too often, we compare ourselves to others without realizing that we are unique and make unique contributions to the lives of others. When we compare ourselves to others or don't meet the unreasonable expectations we set for ourselves, we create negative and self-limiting thoughts. Speaking negatively about yourself limits you from achieving your potential.

For example, when I first joined CrossFit, the only reason I didn't attend the workouts six days a week was because I told myself that working out six days a week would be too much for me. The funny thing is, when I changed my thinking and convinced myself that I *was* capable of working out six days a week, I started to do just that.

I see two types of negative self-talk. The first is when you express negative attitudes about yourself. Things such as:

"I am too fat..." instead of... "I will make

better food choices."

"I am too slow…" rather than… "I am going to work on increasing my speed."

"I don't know enough…" instead of… "I am not sure, so I'll research it."

Repeating negative thoughts prevents you from taking action. You tell yourself what you *can't* do, and then you believe these lies. The only way to overcome inertia is to take action.

The second type of negative self-talk is beating yourself up over decisions that didn't produce the desired results. Years ago, when I was passed over for a promotion, I convinced myself that something I did *not* do caused me to lose the promotion. It didn't matter that I was rated "1," the highest rating I could receive as a consultant. I couldn't let it go. It didn't matter how much anyone told me that I provided great value to my firm. I believed it was *my fault* that I didn't get promoted. The fact that promotions were politically motivated was not about to change my mind. I believed there was something wrong with me. I convinced myself that I wasn't *worthy* of promotion, which impacted the rest of my career at that company.

Eventually, I reframed the things I said about myself. I went from feeling unworthy to saying things such as, "My firm is lucky to have me," "I provide great value to my clients," and "I am a leader of teams and have demonstrated this for years." Reframing my self-talk prompted me to look for a promotion outside of my firm. This paid off when I was later offered a position at another company – a job commensurate with my leadership skills and talents.

Speaking negatively about yourself seems absurd, but we all do it. How often do you say negative things about yourself – statements you would never tolerate if someone else said them? Would you say the negative things you say about yourself to another person? If you answered *no*, then why in the world do you say them to yourself? You should be your own best friend. You should be speaking to and about yourself in only the most glowing terms.

I'm still not completely free from negative self-talk. In fact, I catch myself sharing limiting beliefs with myself on a daily basis. Most often, this happens during CrossFit. Sometimes, I tell myself that I can't lift a certain weight. Then my coach will come over and tell me that I *can* lift heavier. I try it and discover that he was right.

I'm a work in progress. As such, when I recognize that I'm telling myself something negative, or I find myself anxious about my abilities, I tell myself over and over, "You can do this. At least *try* to do this. If you don't try, then it confirms you can't do it."

Avoiding negative self-talk + resilience

If you want to achieve your heart's desires, you have to believe you can. Your mind is set up to obey your commands. If you say you can't do something, then you won't do it.

In *The Power of the Subconscious Mind*, Dr. Joseph Murphy says, "You give the command or decree, and your subconscious mind reproduces the idea impressed upon it."[ix] If you're wondering why the things you tell yourself actually come true, this is why. If you are always saying that you can never be on time, you will absolutely never be on time. Try telling yourself that you *will* make it on time.

[ix] Murphy, Joseph (1963). Mansfield Center, CT. *The Power of the Subconscious Mind*. Martino Publishing

Get started now

❖ Start saying nice things about, and to, yourself. For example, when you catch yourself saying something like "I am a horrible a cook," change that to, "I am in the process of learning to be a better cook."

❖ Check out the tools and resources section for additional reading on the subconscious mind.

— 8 —

Get Help

"If you want to go fast, go alone. If you want to go far, go together."
—*African Proverb*

When I first started writing this chapter, I was going to recommend that you hire a coach. I grew conflicted about that advice because "help" involves much more than coaching. Getting help can mean talking with a friend, visiting a therapist or even asking a stranger for assistance. My point is: we are not meant to face life's challenges alone.

Sadly, many people don't accept this.

I used to be one of them.

Until four years ago, my ego refused to accept help. To my mind, asking for help would have: (a) proved that I was incompetent; and (b) put me in someone else's debt.

Do you ever wonder why some people succeed at accomplishing their goals? Or why some people seem to have it all together? Do you sometimes think, "I can't believe that Susan keeps getting promoted? Is she really that talented? Are her ideas actually better than mine?"

How about your friend who struggled with her weight for years, and then lost 25 pounds in four months? What do you think changed?

Chances are, these people achieved success because they sought help. They either hired the help or they enlisted someone in their life to help them. Or maybe they bought a book or purchased a course that lets them access a "coach" whenever they need one.

Think about your own life. What happened the last time you set a goal of losing 10 pounds or declared that you would pay off your student loan debt? (If you achieved your goals without a hitch, you are amazing. You already know the value of obtaining help, so you may want to skip to the next chapter.) What about the time you were betrayed or your best-laid plans were suddenly derailed? How did it feel? Did you get past it? How? If you haven't gotten past it, how often do these failures creep into your mind? Do they cause you to lose sleep?

Because our egos are so fragile, admitting that we aren't perfect can make us feel inept. To get the help we need, therefore, we have to get out of our own way.

Just last year, I was forced to admit my incompetence in many areas in my life.

First, I admitted that I needed help with

physical fitness, so I joined CrossFit. I show up, and they tell me what I should be doing for the next hour.

Then, I hired a business coach to help me with blogging and building my website: www.simply-resilient.com. Before hiring the coach, I spent almost two years tinkering with the site without much progress to show for it. My coach has gotten me "unstuck." In addition to helping me finish the site, he encouraged me to write this book.

I also found help to cope with the death of my marriage. I needed to understand how and why this could have happened. I was hurt, and I needed to talk with someone who wouldn't judge me. I wanted someone to guide me through the feelings of loss.

Today, I understand the value of seeking help – paid or otherwise. Getting help may cost money, or it may not. If money is an issue, I suggest you identify a friend, relative or colleague who's achieved something that you want to achieve, and then ask the person if they can help you achieve the same goal. If necessary, you can barter services with them. It's entirely possible that *you* could help them achieve a goal with which they've been struggling. (Paying for services – in cash or barter – comes with a big advantage: you're more likely to follow through when the help *costs* something than when it's free.)

Let me be clear about one thing, though. Simply getting someone to help you will not solve your problems. You have to commit to the work they suggest, especially if they aren't charging for their services. If you don't do the work, you're wasting everyone's time.

Getting help + resilience

There is a verse in the Bible (Ecclesiastes) that says, "The thing that hath been, it is that which shall be; and that which is done is that which shall be done and there is no new thing under the sun." In other words, there's nothing you can experience in your life that someone else has not already experienced. For that reason, the best way to meet your challenges is to find someone who has successfully met the same (or similar) challenges.

Get started now

❖ Add 30 minutes in your schedule to perform the following exercise.

Answer the following questions:

1. It is a dream of mine to _____ (lose 15 pounds, start a non-profit, travel to Paris, launch a business, write a book).
2. Why is this my dream?
3. If I achieve this dream, how will it make me feel?
4. How can I get started on the dream?
5. Who do I know that has been successful in this area?
6. How can I get help from them?

— 9 —

Protect Your Time

"Focus on being productive instead of busy."
—Tim Ferris

I used to think that the most valuable currency was cash. However, my cancer diagnosis shifted my perspective. It forced me to ponder how limited my time may be in this life.

Earlier, I mentioned how I once spent loads of time staying busy, which I now know was a mismanagement of my time. I didn't pay attention to the return on investment or the costs vs. benefits of all the activities that kept me busy. I never considered how time spent today would translate into some sort of future benefit. For example, how would chairing a volunteer organization's committee add value to my life next year?

I considered it a badge of honor to be busy for every waking hour. You name it, I did it. I took leadership positions in volunteer organizations, I partied with my friends, watched marathons of reality TV shows, and spent hours on the phone talking about work and celebrities. Looking back, I realize that most of those activities were nothing but a distraction from what I really needed to be doing. I was not proactively managing my time.

I eventually found myself burned out, unfulfilled and on the brink of a mental breakdown. This caused me to evaluate what I was doing and why. My conclusion: most of what I did was random and pointless. Most of my time was being sucked into a black hole that left me feeling unfulfilled. Have you ever heard the saying, "Look at a person's calendar and you can see where their priorities are?" Well, if you looked at my calendar, you wouldn't be able to tell where my priorities were. It was stuffed with random activities and lots of blank spaces, which perpetuated the randomness and contributed to my stress. My life was pulling me in different directions, but I wasn't directing my life.

To protect my time, I implemented four behaviors. These behaviors were life-changing. They immediately brought me peace of mind and reduced the stress and anxiety of feeling pulled in different directions.

Time blocking

Creating time blocks helped me place *intention* on how I spent my time. It improved my self-esteem because, even when I simply watched a Netflix marathon, that time block was now a *planned* relaxation activity, not random "filler."

I started assigning time caps to almost every activity. For example, if I wanted to unwind with Netflix, I might allot three hours for the activity. This helped me feel less guilty about being "unproductive." It also kept me from letting my time slip into a black hole – e.g., letting a few hours of TV turn into an entire day. Don't get me wrong: I don't map out my schedule to the last minute. There are still spontaneous moments and times when – if I'm enjoying myself – I grant myself permission to keep doing whatever I'm doing. But these are exceptions to the rule.

Scheduling phone conversations

I also began managing the amount of time spent talking to friends and family on the phone. This may seem odd, especially in an era when texting is the preferred communication tool, but I like to catch up with people by phone. Since I was a child, and my family can attest to this, time evaporates like a puddle in the Sahara whenever I'm on the phone. To keep this from happening on a too-regular basis, I started scheduling specific days for phone conversations. And for unplanned conversations, I set a cap of 30 minutes. I chose 30 minutes because I found it was just enough time to catch up with a loved one without veering into chatter that really doesn't matter.

Reevaluating how time is spent

My third behavior change was to reevaluate my activities and align them with my goals. My first decision was to surrender my responsibilities in my sorority. This wasn't easy. I had been active in my sorority for 14 years, and volunteering was important to me. However, as time passed, I realized that the organization's goals were no longer aligned with what I wanted, so I replaced the time spent there (and in some other organizations) with one-on-one mentorships that better fulfilled my desire to serve.

Today, whenever I find myself complaining about an activity, I recognize this as a sign that I'm no longer receiving fulfillment from the activity. When that happens, I reevaluate the current and future benefits of continuing to pursue that activity and proceed accordingly.

Using the word "no"

The final tool that I adopted was learning to say "no." Saying "no" also didn't come easy (at first) because I like being there for people. I feel guilty when I think I've let someone down. I eventually had to accept, however, was that somebody – somewhere – would always have an agenda for my time, with no regard for the other activities I wanted in my life. I also had to accept that I couldn't be everywhere, and do everything, at once. If the choice was burning out and keeping everyone "happy" versus eliminating some activities and avoiding a nervous breakdown, I decided to choose the latter. To preserve my sanity – and align my energy with my current goals – I learned to say "no" some of the time.

Protecting your time + resilience

In Maslow's hierarchy of needs, self-actualization is at the top of the pyramid. Self-actualization is the need for personal growth and discovery that is present throughout a person's life. Personal growth and achieving goals contribute to positive self-worth. When we don't achieve our goals or spend time feeling regret for not pursuing personal growth, this can lead to negative thoughts and low self-esteem. Negative thoughts that go unchecked can also lead to depression. When you protect your time, you set yourself up to be more successful in pursuing personal growth. When you protect your time, you are being more intentional. You are taking control of your time and, thereby, your life.

Get started now

❖ Block 30 minutes or an hour of time to review your calendar:
  • What kind of activities appear most often on your calendar?
❖ Start blocking time on Sunday to review your calendar for the week. Scrutinize every entry on the calendar using the following framework, which I call "WIN":
  • **W**ill this activity bring me a future benefit?
  • **I**s there any blank space? If so, what can I do with the time that will bring me enjoyment or future benefits?
  • Would saying "**N**o" to this activity offer any benefits to my life? For example, if you said "no" to the activity, could you get more sleep or spend time accomplishing a more important task?

—10—

Reflect, Reflect, Reflect

"The unexamined life is not worth living."
—Socrates

When was the last time you contemplated the decisions you've made to get to this moment in your life? When was the last time you asked yourself what you want your life to look like in the future and considered which decisions you should make *now* to get there?

Do you know what happens when you don't reflect? You allow inertia to take over. You drift. You stay in an unfulfilling job with minimal raises and no chance for growth. You maintain relationships that should have ended years ago.

I started reflecting while undergoing cancer treatment, which gave me 10 months away from work. I found a journal that I'd purchased a few years earlier, and I noticed (maybe) three entries in there. I became intrigued by the person I was when I wrote those entries. I figured I would start journaling my experience with cancer treatment as a way to reflect on that period after I was finished. What I discovered during this process, however, was that it caused me to more deeply explore my actions by asking and answering questions in the journal. Also, I started to make a habit of looking back at the entries to see how my outlook was changing.

I also used this opportunity to reflect on what went wrong in my marriage. Reflecting on that relationship wasn't easy because I had to face the worst parts of myself. Through these reflections, I discovered that I was complicit in the failure of my marriage, and I identified areas where I could have been a better wife. Going through this process of examining my life helped me discover how I could become a better mate in a future relationship. It also helped me learn what I really want in mate.

I used reflection to figure out what I want from life. Starting my blog, "Simply Resilient," was an idea born of time that was spent reflecting. As a result of beating cancer, I learned so much about being strong that I wanted to share my experience.

Today, time devoted to reflection is an ingrained habit. I reflect by writing in my journal and answering questions about specific areas of my life. For example, I regularly ask if I am happy with my life and the people in it. I also ask if I am happy with the actions I am taking with my health, career and relationships. Based on the answers, I make adjustments. But the questioning doesn't stop there. Once I land on the first answer, I use a technique I learned in business school that is part of "root cause analysis." (Only a nerd like me would use something learned in business school as a self-help aid.)

My reflection usually unfolds like this:

Are you happy with where you are in life? No.

Why not? Because I'm tired all the time.

Why am I tired? Because I'm not sleeping through the night.

Why am I not sleeping through the night? I'm worried that I'll miss a deadline at work.

Why am I worried about missing the deadline? It would reflect badly on me.

Why are you worried about that? Because I want a raise and a promotion, and I need a perfect performance to get those things.

Through reflection, I discovered the *root cause* of why I wasn't sleeping. I was worried about getting a raise and a promotion. I use this exercise of root cause analysis each time I find myself anxious about something.

A less time-consuming way to reflect, especially if you're not interested in journaling (though I highly recommend it), is to make a daily or weekly practice of asking yourself a set of questions that will bring you comfort. For example, "Did I learn anything this week? Have I influenced anyone today? Did I try my best?"

Reflecting + resilience:

When you don't examine your life, you may not know what you're doing and why. You may find yourself on a hamster wheel instead of moving forward. Work and weekends; work and weekends. No long-term plans. No long-term goals. No sense of meaning.

Reflection stimulates our mind, helping us find greater purpose and meaning. Through contemplation, we gain greater control of our destinies. For example, you may wonder why you never have any money to save after paying the bills. If you take a moment to reflect on your finances, you may realize that you simply aren't earning enough and need a side hustle. Or, you might conclude that you're spending too much on Happy Hour drinks.

Get started now

- ❖ Grab a notepad and ask yourself the following:
    - Am I happy with my health right now? Why or why not?
    - Are the five people closest to me adding value or stress to my life?
    - Am I happy with my current work? Why or why not?
- ❖ Before you go to bed tonight, and over the next seven nights, write down five things that went well today and five things you would have done differently.

—11—

Get Your Finances
Under Control

"Financial peace isn't the acquisition of stuff. It's learning to live on less than you make, so you can give money back and have money to invest. You can't win until you do this."
—Dave Ramsey

Gaining control of my finances has brought me great peace of mind. In my opinion, financial stress is the worst kind of stress because it locks you into situations you don't want. For example, you're still married to someone you no longer love because you're in debt together or you created a lifestyle that you can't afford without the other person's income.

Money also ties you to jobs that you hate.

Financial insecurity fuels an endless cycle of anxiety and depression. You're anxious because you don't know how you'll pay the bills. You're depressed because you can't figure out how you ended up here. Well, I've been there, and it's not fun. My biggest financial blunders were trying to "keep up with the Joneses" (also known as living beyond your means) and FOMO (Fear of Missing Out). Both mistakes can be traced to my lack of financial discipline.

Like many Americans, I graduated from college with a lot of student loan debt and credit card debt. I started my adult life trying to keep up with the Joneses. By the time I landed my first job, I was already behind financially. My debt had already staked a big claim to my salary. I also lacked the know-how and the tools to maintain a budget.

After a year of working that first job out of college, I hated my life. I was commuting two and half hours a day and working with someone I hated. This was my first experience with feeling trapped. Every day, I would head to work seething with anger at myself for being in debt and being stuck in a job I hated because of it. I also felt incompetent because I didn't know how to escape. How could that be? I was a college-educated woman with a degree in accounting. How could I not know how to manage my own finances?

I was able to pay down my debt with my ex-husband's help a few years later, but that wasn't the end of bad financial decisions. In 2006, right after we got married, we bought a house with an interest-only mortgage in order to keep up with the Joneses and because, as newlyweds, we were under so much outside pressure to start a family. In 2009, these decisions came back to haunt us. I found myself commuting to another job I hated while our house depreciated in value, thanks to the housing bust. I lived in a perpetual state of anxiety because: (1) I was being bullied by my direct manager; and (2) I was afraid to lose my job, given the terrible state of the economy. My anxiety was so bad that the mere thought of going to work produced insomnia and gastro-intestinal problems. But I had to go. I needed to pay the bills.

I eventually quit that awful job, but experiences like these were what I needed. They convinced me to develop a system for managing my finances. After trying all sorts of budgeting apps, like mint.com, I discovered that what worked best for me was tracking my expenses with old-fashioned Microsoft Excel and then automating my savings, bill paying and investments.

Tracking my expenses was valuable because it brought awareness of what I was spending the money on. When I first started doing this, I discovered I was spending at least $200 a month on gifts for other people. This usually happened when someone had a birthday, a baby or a wedding. This may sound selfish, but I became irritated by this discovery because it was usually an unexpected cash outlay. When I was budgeting, I never thought, "Joan is having a baby. I should put some money aside for a gift." Today, I do exactly that. I came up with a line item in my budget for unexpected gifts. Had I not tracked my expenses, I would have never noticed how much I was spending on other people.

Automating your expenses

Spending a few hours a month to pay bills and adjust my savings had always been stressful. I was too busy with work to spend time figuring out which bill was due on which date. To mitigate the stress, I set up automatic deductions from my accounts to take care of my living expenses, savings and investments. Automating your finances is a total mindset shift. It may be awkward at first, but as the months go by, you'll realize that the energy you once devoted to stressing out can now be applied to more productive pursuits.

Today, I *obsess* over my finances, but I don't *stress out* over them. I review my budget every week. I know where every dollar is going, but I no longer worry about making ends meet.

Get Started Now

- ❖ Transfer downloaded bank statements and credit card statements from your online accounts into an Excel format.
- ❖ Sort your expenses by vendor to get a better idea of where you're spending your money, as well as what your total expenses are.
- ❖ Once you've arrived at the total expense figure, create a budget in Excel (there's an example in the **Tools and Resources** section of this book) or set up your budget at mint.com. See the **Tools and Resources** section for more budgeting options.
- ❖ In your budget, make sure you identify the following:
  - Income – Your paycheck + any side hustle income.
  - All of your fixed expenses (rent, mortgage, utilities, phone, student loans).
  - Your variable expenses (clothing, food, entertainment, gifts).
  - How much you want to allot for savings.
  - How much you want to allot for investments.

- ❖ If you don't have automatic savings set up, based on what's left over in your budget or your goals for savings, set up a savings account that automatically deducts your desired dollar amount every month.
- ❖ If you have enough left over for investments, I recommend you read "Brass Knuckle Finance" by one of my college mates, Jarim Person-Lynn.[x]

---

[x] Person-Lynn, Jarim (2016). *Brass Knuckle Finance*

—12—

Your Network
Creates Your Net Worth

**"When you know people, and those people
know what you do, success knows how to find
you."**
—Kelly Hoey

Creating and nurturing my network is probably the most valuable action I've taken in my adult life. When I speak of networking, I'm not referring to social networking on LinkedIn, Facebook and Instagram. I'm referring to good old fashioned "meeting and greeting" with live humans. Social media can be a great place to *virtually* meet, but it's no substitute for meeting and talking with people in person. In fact, whenever you meet someone on social media, I encourage you to connect with that new acquaintance in person, whenever possible, especially if you're planning to invest a lot of time in the relationship. There is nothing more powerful than an actual human-to-human connection.

Don't get me wrong: I *have* met people on social media who have helped me address certain issues. But my best connections have been made through face-to-face meetings.

The other reason I'm not a fan of

cultivating a network through social media is because many people spend a *lot* of time curating their profiles. Thanks to this, it's difficult to discern who a person really is. (If Facebook and Instagram had been around in the 1930s, Hitler might have had a profile featuring vegetarian recipes and funny cat videos.) In person, on the other hand, you can study someone's body language, tone of voice and facial expressions to get a more accurate sense of their personality and motives. It's hard to fake those things.

Most people find networking intimidating. It's funny because when we were children, most of us were forced to play with kids we never met before, and I personally don't remember being anxious about it. As an adult, I determined that my intimidation stemmed from fear of rejection and embarrassment. I would worry that I'd greet someone new and then be rudely ignored. This has actually happened a few times, but I've come to realize that I can't let these statistically insignificant encounters prevent me from growing my network.

Now that I know this about myself, I don't worry about rejection. Instead, I create a strategy for the networking events I attend. The strategy isn't fancy. I set a goal of connecting with a minimum of five people. I use five as the goal because I'm a deep connector, and setting a goal larger than five would put me under pressure to engage in shorter conversations. In addition, I come prepared with two questions for everyone I meet: (1) "What brought you to this event?" and (2) "What do you do for a living, and what's your side passion?" The answers help me decide if a potential relationship might be beneficial. They also help me determine how I might be of help to the person.

Nurturing a network changed my life, allowing me to achieve goals I could not have attained otherwise. I got my first job after college because of networking. I began networking as an undergraduate after joining the National Association of Black Accountants (NABA). Each year, NABA hosts a conference that offers members the opportunity to submit their resumes to top accounting firms and Fortune 500 companies. During one of the conferences, I earned an internship with a school district, where I built a relationship with the controller. Eventually, the controller became a partner at a small accounting firm.

Building this relationship through NABA proved valuable because, when I graduated college, the accounting industry was not doing well. At the time, the reputation of public accounting was suffering, and one of the largest accounting firms had lost its license to practice. To say the least, this made it challenging for recent grads to find work in the field. So I reached out to the controller I had worked with. I knew she had gone to a small firm so I asked if they had any positions open. They did not. Then. But eight months later, she emailed to say that a position had opened up. I went for an interview and was hired.

Without this network, who knows what would have happened? That opportunity was the catalyst for my career. Since then, every job I've landed started with a network-related introduction.

Networking + resilience

Nurturing your network can bring resilience to your career and finances. But don't take my word for it. Ask friends who love their jobs how they got them. I'll bet most will say that they knew someone in the company who passed along their resume. Networking can also be helpful in other areas. For example, you may not be looking for a job yourself, but maybe you're looking to hire someone. Or, maybe you're moving to a new city and could use the advice of a local who knows something about the real estate market and the employment situation there.

Get started now:

❖ This week, send a note to three people in your network. The note could be a simple as you checking in with them, or you can send an article that they might find interesting.

❖ Visit www.meetup.com, or get the app and find a topic of interest. Once you've found something, attend that event with the intention of making two connections.

—13—

Protect Yourself
from Toxic People

**"Energy is contagious: either you affect people
or you infect people."**
—*T. Harv Eker*

You can't avoid toxic people. There are simply too many of them in this world. But you *can* learn to manage your interactions with them.

A toxic person is someone who brings negative energy into your space. They're pretty easy to spot. They're the ones who always complain and never accept responsibility for their actions. In my experience, toxic people are generally good people who don't realize their effect on others – or themselves. However, I've also known some who were horrible people *and* horribly toxic. These folks are so broken that they just don't care how their behavior affects anyone. If you encounter either type, you need to be prepared.

What makes me qualified to offer advice on this topic?

I used to be a toxic person.

I transformed myself into a toxic person while working at my first job. My life at the time consisted of a two-and-a-half-hour commute (round trip) on days when I was actually in the office. When I was traveling for the job, it could involve stretches of up to six weeks, five days a week. My health was going down the toilet because I wasn't eating well while I was on the road. To top it off, my *boss* was a toxic person. She nitpicked and second-guessed me all day, every day.

When I think back to that time, all I did was complain. Anytime I got someone to listen, whether in person or on the phone, I complained. My outlook was very dark. I was in my early twenties, and was so self-unaware that I didn't see what I'd become. People would say to me, "Stop complaining" or "Why are you always so negative" or "If you hate your job so much, why don't you leave?" I know now that I'd become toxic, but these comments didn't register with me back then. All I knew was that I didn't feel in control of my life. I hated my job, but I needed the job to pay my bills, so I hated *myself* for staying there.

Today, I only occasionally become toxic, often after being around a toxic person. I usually recognize this because my energy will be low and I'll feel sadness or anger when there's nothing to be sad or angry about.

Sometimes, I don't recognize the problem myself, but because I have such a wonderful tribe around me – people who aren't afraid to critique me – they will tell me that my mood is crap and that I need to meditate.

I recently had to handle a toxic client. The experience was quite shocking. I hadn't encountered someone this horrible in many years. Her toxicity symptoms included: failing to take responsibility for any of her actions; challenging me and my team for the sake of challenging us; throwing us under the bus; name calling and belittling. She was a first-class jerk, but I couldn't walk away from her.

Instead, I implemented these self-care tactics to survive the situation – tactics I now implement whenever I encounter a toxic person, especially if prolonged exposure is likely.

Bring joy to your day, every day

To manage the effects of toxic people, practice bringing joy to your day. Figure out what you can do on a daily basis, or most days, that will make you happy. For me, that is exercise. When dealing with the toxic client, I made a commitment to do CrossFit every day for six days in a row. I worked out early in the morning, and was so full of joy and energy afterward that any negativity that later came my way bounced off me. That positive energy became my armor.

Set an intention for the day

At the beginning of yoga, the instructor tells us to set an intention for our practice, and I usually achieve this intention. I've applied this lesson to my personal life to help gain control of my days. Before leaving home in the morning, I set intentions for what I want to accomplish. I literally look at a list and say out loud: "Today, I'm going to finish the report, and I will meet with Sally, Joe and Suzy to go over it." Setting this intention helps me accomplish everything I want to achieve that day. I become so focused on accomplishing my intentions that I'm not fazed by background noise or the games that toxic people play.

Journal

Ever since cancer treatment, journaling has been a life saver. On days when I'm living in my head, with all sorts of thoughts swirling around, journaling has brought me peace and prompted me to reflect. On especially bad days – e.g., because of encounters with toxic people – I journal about my day before going to bed. This helps me unpack my emotions and analyze *why* I am experiencing them. Because I'm a problem solver, I identify ways to fix my problems by putting them on paper. In this way, I either figure out a way to solve my problem or I decide that it didn't really matter and move on.

Meditation

Because I'm only human, I sometimes decide that I don't need meditation anymore because I'm perfectly fine. That's my ego talking. And when I hear the ego saying things like that, it's usually time to up my meditation game, especially if I've had recent interactions with toxic people. When you're dealing with a toxic person, a consistent meditation practice can be a very effective shield against their behavior – behavior that could otherwise bring you down.

Protecting yourself from toxic people + resilience

Being in the presence of a toxic person puts you at risk of becoming toxic. Exposure to that kind of negativity can make you feel trapped. That feeling can lead to depression, and once depression takes hold, who knows where it will lead?

Get started now

❖ Identify the toxic people in your space. If certain people leave you feeling, sad, angry or defensive, they're usually toxic. Once you know who they are, enlist some of the self-care tools mentioned above.

❖ When you identify a toxic person, don't fall into their trap of endless negative exchanges. That will only leave you frustrated and depleted of energy.

14

Be Selective About Who You Keep in Your Squad

"You are the average of the five people you spend your time with."
—Jim Rohn

When I talk about your squad, I'm referring to the people who have a seat at your table, which is very different than your network. The people with a seat at your table are the people you meet with and talk with regularly about what's happening in your life. These people will have the greatest impact on you because they are the ones who will introduce you to your next sale or job, share an article that may change your life, or hold a mirror to your face when you need to change. These are the people who want to see you happy, who want nothing but the best for you. That circle of people cannot include just anyone.

My inner circle has changed over and over. I've let some people go, and demoted others to the outer circles. This isn't because I'm an asshole, but because I assessed the value I was adding to that person's life versus the value I was receiving. As I discussed in Chapter 8, you can't let everyone have access to your time. (And to be clear, a demotion merely means they will be interacting with you less often. It doesn't necessarily mean that you care about them any less.)

I have always had the desire for more in my life, and over the years, I learned that if I want to elevate my lifestyle – have a higher income, a more challenging job or more education – I need to be exposed to people who have achieved (or are in the process of achieving) the things I desire. For that reason, the composition of my squad has changed about 10 times. And it usually changes based on whatever new things I'm trying to achieve.

The most drastic change I made to my squad was when I decided to get my MBA. Prior to that, my squad was a couple of friends from work, a few of my sorority sisters, my ex-husband and my family. Once I started grad school and the work encroached on my free time, a new squad emerged. The new squad comprised of my classmates and my ex-husband. School was the most important thing in my life at the time, and I immersed myself in everything school-related. Even when I socialized, it was with my classmates. After I graduated, my squad continued evolving to reflect my changing goals, desires and priorities.

When selecting a squad, first be clear about what you want in life. If you aren't clear, you may find yourself collecting random people and goals (if any), and living a life of mediocrity. For example, I'm currently prioritizing enjoyment and positive life experiences. If you were to look at my squad now, you'd see that it includes my CrossFit squad, my travel buddies, a weekly social crew and my business coach, as well as folks to whom I frequently reach out as a sounding board for big life decisions (such as my mom and my bestie). My friends who no longer live in the same city as me often say that I'm "living my best life" or "this fun and amazing life." That's because I decided to form a squad that promotes a good life but also keeps me grounded, encouraging me to achieve the things I've set out to accomplish.

A selective squad + resilience

Why should you be choosy about your squad? Because the people closest to you will either influence you to be better, help you maintain the status quo or bring you down. I've watched those shows on addiction, and one of the things the counselors tell addicts is to avoid their old crew – the "people, places and things" that could trigger a relapse.

To be more selective about the people with whom you spend time, ask yourself, "Is this person's lifestyle in alignment with what I want my lifestyle to be?" For example, if you want to be fit and healthy, surround yourself with people who are health-conscious.

Get started now

❖ Block an hour this week to gain clarity about what you want in your life. Use the NIIT framework that I've developed (below) to assist you:
  - **N**etwork - Who do I know that has been successful in this area?
  - **I**mportance - Why do I want this thing in my life now?
  - **I**mpact - How will this thing impact my life?
  - **T**ime – Do I have the time to commit to making this thing happen?

❖ Once you've completed the framework and have gained clarity on what you want in your life, reach out to the person you identified in your network, and schedule a time to talk with them about their success in this area. Come prepared with questions. Also, take to the internet to research the topic in which you're interested, then, be proactive about spending more time around your role model (or models). For instance, if you want a better body, consider skipping that boozy brunch in favor of a workout at the gym with your role model.

15

Be You, Do You

"Today you are you that is truer than true. There is no one who is alive who is youer than you."
—*Dr. Seuss*

These days, people are always talking about how they want to be happy, and the one commonality I see among people who desire happiness is that they aren't living their own lives. When I look back at my life, I break it into three phases: (1) learning; (2) un-learning; and (3) re-learning how to live. Some of us never make it all way to the third phase, but those who *do* are probably living the happiest life they've ever experienced.

My learning phase involved a lot of conformity to our culture. Because American culture is consumerist and capitalist, I spent the better part of my life learning to integrate into that culture, believing that success and happiness were measured by the money I made and the things I acquired.

So when I was very young, I set out to achieve the American dream. I decided to go to college because I was told that I wouldn't amount to anything without a degree. I selected accounting as a major because I learned that becoming a CPA would give me a decent salary. The conforming continued when I joined professional organizations, where I was taught how to act, dress and think in my future workplaces.

I learned from our culture that getting married and having kids was the ultimate sign of success – and I wanted to be successful. I got the husband and I got the house. We both had well-paying jobs. I even managed to fit in an MBA because I learned that I could secure an even higher income by entering a network of fellow MBAs in high positions. I had it all, except for the kids. But I still wasn't happy.

How could this be? I played by the rules and followed the conventional wisdom.

About this time, I decided to "Do Me" by leaving my marriage. Thus began my unlearning phase. I was scared to death of leaving my marriage, even though I was miserable. I had spent so much time conforming that I didn't want to disappoint the people who believed in me. I worried how my former advisors would react to the girl who seemed so successful at everything but marriage.

After spending my life trying to fit in,

becoming an "authentic me" wasn't easy. Plenty of people wanted me to stay the same – to be the person they'd always known. When you enter the unlearning phase, your friends and family may shame and ridicule you. When I got divorced, I lost a heap of friends, but the upside of losing those friends was that I gained better friends – people who truly care about me and support who I *really* am.

During this phase, I also noticed that I no longer liked where I worked and what I was doing. I didn't realize how quickly my process of un-conforming was happening until I started to have a lot of negative interactions at work. Initially, I couldn't put my finger on what was different. I was doing great work, which was reflected in my performance reviews, but I no longer had strong relationships with people. In a moment of reflection, I realized that I'd outgrown the people I worked with. I no longer had a passion for what I was doing. It was time for me to move on. Coming to this realization wasn't easy. I worked in my firm for nearly eight years, and always thought it would be my ultimate career destination.

My decision to "Do Me" in my personal life had seeped into my professional life, and I am better for it.

Today, I've entered a transitional phase as I near the end of the unlearning stage and ramp up for the re-learning phase. I haven't yet left the un-learning phase because I think there are still some cultural norms I haven't yet jettisoned.

In the re-learning phase, I will figure out who I am and who I want to be. Re-learning who I am will mean discovering that everyone is allowed to live their life the way they want – free of judgement. In the re-learning phase, I will learn that many of the choices I made were made because of fear – fear of being different. In the phase of re-learning, I will become okay with being different.

I wish I could offer you a step-by-step guide on how to "Do You." All I can say is that you will have to reach a point where you decide *exactly* what you want. You will have to decide that you don't care if someone gets upset with you for doing what's best for you, your family and your mental health. You will reach decisions that aren't based on outside pressure or the fear of disappointing friends and family. You will come to a point where you are no longer afraid of what people might say about you.

There is no how-to guide for being you and

doing you. You just have to be brave and decide to change. You also must be ready for the backlash from people in your life. That's okay, because you are the one who has to live with you.

I believe many of us are suffering because we all have learned to be what society wants, even when a small voice inside implores us to become who we really are. When we work up the nerve to do that, the fear inside us can take over. "What if she leaves me? What if I get fired? What if I get a bad review? What if I get rejected?" These are all valid questions, but what you should also be adding to those questions is, "So what if she leaves me? How will my life be better if I do this? How will my kid's life be better if I leave him?"

Being you and doing you + resilience

If you are not being and doing the things your heart truly wants, you are living an unhappy life. This life is often riddled with depression, not lasting and genuine fulfillment. I've read countless articles and listened to weeks' worth of podcasts about nurses who work with the dying and the most common regrets the dying have. One article from

Business Insider was written by Susie Stein. She interviewed a palliative nurse, who summarized the Top 5 things that people regret most on their death beds. They are:

1. I wish I had the courage to live a life true to myself, not the life others expected of me.
2. I wish I hadn't worked so hard.
3. I wish I'd had the courage to express my feelings.
4. I wish I'd stayed in touch with my friends.
5. I wish I'd let myself be happier.[xi]

Notice that two of those regrets are about having the courage to be yourself and express who you truly are.

If anything, *being you* and *doing you* can lead to a life of happiness and fewer regrets.

[xi] Steiner, Susie (2013 December 5) *The 5 Things Most People Regret on Their Deathbed*. www.businessinsider.com

Get started now

❖ Block an hour of time this week to answer these questions:

  o What is one thing I wish I had more courage to say or do? Ask yourself why you don't have the courage to say or do that thing, and determine if the fear is rational.

  o Is there something you've always wanted to do, but you worry about being ridiculed by the most important people in your life?

   ▪ Is this fear rational?

   ▪ What is the worst thing that would happen if you went ahead and did it?

   ▪ Are you willing to live with the worst-case scenario?

  o Are you doing something because someone else expects you to do it, even though you get no pleasure from this activity?

   ▪ If yes, ask yourself if (and why) this expectation lowers your energy or negatively affects your mood.

   ▪ Ask yourself, "Is the expectation reasonable?"

- Ask yourself, "Does this expectation bring any benefit to me?"
- Ask yourself, "What would happen if I quit living up to this expectation? How bad would my life be?"

Epilogue

I hope you enjoyed this book and have found some tools that will improve your life. As you embark on your journey of resilience, keep in mind that it won't be easy. However, as long as you stay consistent and fall in love with the process, you will obtain the results you work for. Living a life of resilience is an ongoing project. There are times when I falter, and when I do, I reach back to the tools I just shared with you to get back on track. I'm not perfect, and the best thing I can do for myself is to forgive myself for falling down. Then get back up and try something new.

I invite you to visit my website www.simply-resilient.com for more stories on resilience. Also, feel free to join my Facebook Community, "Resilience Revolution," which is committed to helping everyone lead a resilient life.

Tools and Resources

Below are lists of resources that I use to live a more resilient life.

Tools and resources, I lean on to rewire my brain for positivity.

Books

- Mediations to Heal Your Life, Louise Hay
- The Happiness Advantage, Shawn Achor

Mobile Apps

- Mindful
- Simple Habits
- Headspace
- 21-Day Meditation

Tools I use to help me take control of, and automate, my finances.

Books

- Brass Knuckle Finance, Jarim Person-Lynn
- I Will Teach You to Be Rich, Ramit Sethi

Mobile Apps

- Mint.com – Budget Tracking
- Acorns – Savings and Investing
- Clarity – Savings

Example of my budget in Excel:

Annual Budget

Income:	January	February	March	April	May	June	July	August	September	October	November	December	Total
Paycheck -Take Home	5,000	5,000	5,000	5,000	5,000	5,000	5,000	5,000	5,000	5,000	5,000	5,000	60,000
Side Hustle	1,000	1,000	1,000	1,000	1,000	1,000	1,000	1,000	1,000	1,000	1,000	1,000	12,000
Other	100	100	100	100	100	100	100	100	100	100	100	100	1,200
Total Income	6,100	6,100	6,100	6,100	6,100	6,100	6,100	6,100	6,100	6,100	6,100	6,100	73,200
Expenses													
Fixed Expenses													
Rent/Mortgage	2,000	2,000	2,000	2,000	2,000	2,000	2,000	2,000	2,000	2,000	2,000	2,000	24,000
Car Payment	325	325	325	325	325	325	325	325	325	325	325	325	3,900
Car Insurance	-	-	-	-	300	-	-	-	-	-	300	-	600
Student Loan	400	400	400	400	400	400	400	400	400	400	400	400	4,800
Gym Membership	100	100	100	100	100	100	100	100	100	100	100	100	1,200
Total fixed expenses	2,825	2,825	2,825	2,825	3,125	2,825	2,825	2,825	2,825	2,825	3,125	2,825	34,500
Variable Expense													
Utilities	210	210	210	210	210	210	210	210	210	210	210	210	2,520
Groceries	350	350	350	350	350	350	350	350	350	350	350	350	4,200
Clothing	-	-	300	-	-	300	-	-	300	-	-	300	1,200
Car Maintenance	-	-	200	-	-	200	-	-	200	-	-	200	800
Gasoline	150	150	150	150	150	150	150	150	150	150	150	150	1,800
Home Goods	60	60	60	60	60	60	60	60	60	60	60	60	720
Restaurants	200	200	200	200	200	200	200	200	200	200	200	200	2,400
Entertainment	200	200	200	200	200	200	200	200	200	200	200	200	2,400
Grooming	250	250	250	250	250	250	250	250	250	250	250	250	3,000
Dry Cleaning/Laundry	40	40	40	40	40	40	40	40	40	40	40	40	480
Contributions	100	100	100	100	100	100	100	100	100	100	100	100	1,200
Membership dues	-	-	-	-	-	-	-	-	-	600	-	-	600
Gifts	50	50	50	50	50	50	50	50	50	50	50	50	600
Total variable expenses	1,610	1,610	2,110	1,610	1,610	2,110	1,610	1,610	2,110	2,210	1,610	2,110	21,920
Total net income (loss)	1,665	1,665	1,165	1,665	1,365	1,165	1,665	1,665	1,165	1,065	1,365	1,165	16,780

Example of my monthly budget vs. actual spending:

	A	B	C	D	E
1	February Budget to Actual				
2					
3					
4	Income:	February	Actuals	Variance	
5	Paycheck -Take Home	5,000	5,125	125	
6	Side Hustle	1,000	950	(50)	
7	Other	100	30	(70)	
8	Total Income	6,100	6,105	5	
9				-	
10				-	
11	**Expenses**			-	
12	*Fixed Expenses*			-	
13	Rent/Mortgage	2,000	2,000	-	
14	Car Payment	325	325	-	
15	Car Insurance	-	-	-	
16	Student Loan	400	400	-	
17	Gym Membership	100	100	-	
18	Total fixed expenses	2,825	2,825	-	
19				-	
10	*Variable Expense*			-	
11	Utilities	210	222	(12)	
12	Groceries	350	360	(10)	
13	Clothing	-	100	(100)	
14	Car Maintenance	-	-	-	
15	Gasoline	150	140	10	
16	Home Goods	60	100	(40)	
17	Restaurants	200	210	(10)	
18	Entertainment	200	250	(50)	
19	Grooming	250	200	50	
10	Dry Cleaning/Laundry	40	-	40	
11	Contributions	100	100	-	
12	Membership dues	-	-	-	
13	Gifts	50	100	(50)	
14	Total variable expenses	1,610	1,782	(172)	
15					
16	Total net income (loss)	1,665	1,498	167	
17					
18					

Books that help me take life a little less seriously and avoid anxious or depressing thoughts.

- High Performance Habits, Brendan Burchard
- The Subtle Art of Not Giving a F*ck, Mark Manson
- Ego Is the Enemy, Ryan Holiday
- Awaken the Giant Within, Anthony Robbins
- The Power of the Subconscious Mind, Joseph Murphy

My favorite tools for journaling and managing my life.

- ✓ Simply Resilient Reflection Journal – Simply-resilient.com
- ✓ The Ink + Volt 2018 Planner Signature Series – www. Inkandvolt.com

Wait, don't go yet! I've got a favor to ask.

I'd like to say thank you for purchasing my book. I am confident if you start using the suggested tools and resources, you will begin to see your confidence increase in the face of adversity. But before you run off to become an awesome resilient human, could you please take 60 seconds to rate and write a quick blurb for my book on Amazon? As an independent author this is the best way to gain more exposure so that I can share my message of resilience to a wider audience. Your 60 second contribution will impact the lives of others in the most positive way.

To post your review please search the title through the Amazon search engine. Thank you for your support.

About the Author

Christmas is a breast cancer survivor and divorcee who has the uncanny ability of handling adversity with grace. Since successfully undergoing cancer treatment and dealing with the grief of her marriage ending, she has made it her life's mission to share with others the tools she uses to remain resilient through life's challenges.

Christmas started her career in accounting and then transitioned into risk consulting, and is now an executive in Human Resources. It was through her experiences at work and her natural ability for coaching and mentoring that she discovered her gift for coaching and challenged herself to expand her audience by starting her blog Simply Resilient, where she shares her experiences both in life and in the workplace.

Outside of the office, Christmas is an avid cross-fitter living in Brooklyn, NY. She is a volunteer mentor of Everwise, and a contributing writer to HuffPost and PIVOT Magazine.

For information on workshops and events please visit www.simply-resilient.com.

To book Christmas to speak at your event or for inquiries scheduling Resilience Lifestyle coaching please email info@simply-resilient.com.

Made in the USA
Monee, IL
28 July 2020